LINCOLN SPEAKS

LINCOLN SPEAKS

WORDS THAT TRANSFORMED A NATION

Richard Carwardine
Declan Kiely
Sandra M. Trenholm

THE MORGAN LIBRARY & MUSEUM, NEW YORK

Exhibition at the Morgan Library & Museum,
New York
23 January–7 June 2015

*Lead funding for this exhibition is provided by
Karen H. Bechtel and the Gilder Foundation,
with additional generous support from Richard and
Ronay Menschel.*

Library of Congress Cataloguing-in-Publication
Data: A catalogue record for this book is available
from the publisher.

ISBN: 978-0-87598-169-7

COVER: Alexander Gardner. Photographic portrait
of Abraham Lincoln, 8 November 1863. The Gilder
Lehrman Institute of American History; GLC00245.

FRONTISPIECE: Matthew Brady. Photographic
portrait of Abraham Lincoln on the day of the
Cooper Union address, 27 February 1860. From a
copy in the collection of Frederick H. Meserve,
New York, 1912. The Morgan Library & Museum;
MA 810.21.

PAGE 21: Timothy O'Sullivan. Five generations of
an African-American family on J. J. Smith's
Plantation, Beaufort, South Carolina, 1862. The
Gilder Lehrman Institute of American History;
GLC05111.01.1038.

PAGE 29 (*clockwise from top left*):
1. Abraham Lincoln. Ambrotype said to have been
made in Macomb, Illinois, 27 August 1858, and last
owned by Richard Watson Gilder. It was destroyed
by fire in 1888. From a copy in the collection of
Frederick H. Meserve, New York, 1912. The
Morgan Library & Museum; MA 810.19.
2. Alexander Hesler. Photographic portrait of
Abraham Lincoln, Chicago, 1858. From a copy in
the collection of Frederick H. Meserve, New York,
1912. The Morgan Library & Museum; MA 810.20.
3. Alexander Gardner. One of the last series of
photographs made by Gardner, Washington, DC,
9 April 1865. From a copy in the collection of
Frederick H. Meserve, New York, 1912. The Morgan Library & Museum; MA 810.27.
4. Alexander Hesler. Photographic portrait of
Abraham Lincoln, Springfield, Illinois, 1860. From
a copy in the collection of Frederick H. Meserve,
New York, 1912. The Morgan Library & Museum;
MA 810.22.

PAGES 38–39: Alexander Gardner. General George
McClellan (left) with President Abraham Lincoln
at McClellan's headquarters in Antietam,
Maryland, 1 October 1862. The Gilder Lehrman
Institute of American History; GLC04346.

PAGE 43: Brady-Handy. Photographic portrait of
Ulysses S. Grant between 1870 and 1880.
The Morgan Library & Museum; MA 1015.

PAGE 58: Charles Gustrine. Broadside, *True Sons of
Freedom*. Chicago, Illinois, 1918. The Gilder
Lehrman Institute of American History; GLC09121.

PAGE 60: Matthew Brady. President Lincoln and
his son Tad, Washington, probably early 1861.
Printed directly from the original negative in the
collection of Frederick H. Meserve, New York,
1912. The Morgan Library & Museum; MA 810.23.

CONTENTS

DIRECTOR'S FOREWORD

No other president in our nation's history has commanded the attention of successive generations as powerfully as Abraham Lincoln has. Venerated from the moment of his assassination 150 years ago, Lincoln is ubiquitous in popular culture and continues to fascinate historians, politicians, playwrights, moviemakers, and novelists.

But the scale of Lincoln's greatness is so monumental that it is sometimes possible to lose sight of the man himself and the means by which he attained his stature. *Lincoln Speaks: Words that Transformed a Nation* looks closely at Lincoln's sensitivity to the power of words and his mastery of the English language. The exhibition traces his boyhood and adult reading, his lifelong enjoyment of poetry and plays, through his public and private letters and several drafts of the magnificent speeches that shaped the course of our country's history. It is organized in the belief that Lincoln speaks as powerfully and eloquently to us now as in his own time, and that his message—and his moral example— remain urgent and necessary.

Developed in partnership with the Gilder Lehrman Institute of American History, whose collaborative spirit and commitment provided endless inspiration, the works in *Lincoln Speaks* are drawn principally from the Morgan's collection of Lincoln letters and manuscripts, the Gilder Lehrman Collection, and the Shapell Manuscript Foundation. This project is made possible by generous gifts from Karen H. Bechtel, the Gilder Foundation, and Richard and Ronay Menschel. I would like to express my profound appreciation to these benefactors. Our gratitude is also due to Professor James G. Basker, Professor Richard Carwardine, Susan F. Saidenberg, and Sandra M. Trenholm.

Peggy Fogelman
Acting Director, The Morgan Library & Museum

INTRODUCTION

Abraham Lincoln delighted in the rich possibilities of language. Throughout his life, he strove to honor the written and spoken word. Largely self-taught, he achieved a literary command that helped him to win the presidency and, once there, to define in memorable prose the purposes that had shaped the nation. No American president has given more eloquent expression to the founding principle of human equality laid out in the Declaration of Independence or used language more forcefully to defend the integrity of the Union and Constitution.

Lincoln penned his own speeches. He chose words with a lawyer's precision and a poet's sense of rhythm, confident of the power of language to persuade an audience. Writing with great deliberation, he used language that was spare, colorful, and accessible to all classes: it seemed to Harriet Beecher Stowe that it had "the relish and smack of the soil." As president, he deployed ethical teaching, painstaking reason, and wry humor; he resisted easy demagoguery and personal abuse. By these means, Lincoln—the common man—reached uncommon heights of eloquence.

I think nothing equals Macbeth.
It is wonderful.

ABRAHAM LINCOLN
17 August 1863

LINCOLN THE READER

The writings that gave Lincoln greatest pleasure also gave direction to his native talent. He read, reread, and absorbed the poetic language of the King James translation of the Bible. Lincoln revered Shakespeare's plays and sonnets for their imagery, metrical rhythms, emotional range, and psychological perception. From memory he could recite long passages from the Bard's tragedies and histories. He appreciated the political oratory of his Whig hero Henry Clay, studied Blackstone's Commentaries on the Laws of England and other legal texts, and mastered books of Euclidean logic. Together these influences confirmed his preference for words that appealed to reason, not mere emotion. In his favorite poem, William Knox's "Mortality"—beginning and ending, "Oh, why should the spirit of mortal be proud?"—Lincoln saw the power of rhythmic repetition. And in the comic thrusts of contemporary humorists and satirists, such as Artemus Ward and David Ross Locke, he saw skill bordering on genius. All in all, Lincoln had no appetite for grandiloquence and pretension. Rather, he admired writing that was clear and cogent, and that, when spoken, was pleasing to the ear.

ABRAHAM LINCOLN

(1809–1865)

Autograph letter, signed, Fremont, to Andrew Johnston, 18 April 1846

Shapell Manuscript Collection; SMF 1553

Lincoln was born only a few weeks after Poe. The author came to his attention
through one of the numerous parodies of "The Raven," first published in January
1845. Johnston, a fellow lawyer, sent Lincoln one such parody, "The Pole-Cat," which
led him to seek out Poe's poem. It is said that Lincoln so appreciated the poem that
he "carried Poe around on the Circuit—read and loved 'The Raven'—repeated it
over & over." This letter—written before Lincoln became familiar with Poe's work—
includes a poem occasioned by a return home in 1844 that "aroused feelings in [him]
which were extremely poetic." Redolent of the dark melancholy that suffuses the
work of his noted contemporary, its final lines read: *And feel (companion of the dead)
/ I'm living in the tombs.*

ABRAHAM LINCOLN

(1809–1865)

"The Bear Hunt," Springfield, ca. 6 September 1846

The Morgan Library & Museum, purchased by Pierpont Morgan, 1905; MA 229.1

Lincoln adored poetry and began composing poems in his teens. He remained an avid reader and writer of verse throughout his life; his last documented poem was written in 1863. He wrote this vivid and comic poem about a bear hunt a month after his election to the U.S. House of Representatives. It may well be "the third canto" that he mentioned in his letter to Johnston on 25 February 1847. Johnston's reason for not selecting this ballad for publication with Lincoln's other poem in the *Quincy Whig* remains unclear. The fourth stanza on the right-hand page reads *But who did this, and how to trace / What's true from what's a lie, / Like lawyers, in a murder case / They stoutly* _argufy._

A house divided against itself can not stand.

THE POLITICIAN

Lincoln's public career coincided with the maturing of a democratic, two-party system marked by boisterous campaigning and torrents of rhetoric. Whether working for his own election or that of others, he showed an aptitude for the new politics and connected easily with the public. In the main he spoke extemporaneously, but he prepared notes for his most important speeches. His faith in people's intelligence and moral sense led him naturally to use logic and reason as means of persuasion. He despised the florid rhetoric associated with Daniel Webster and other celebrated Whig orators of the day, preferring a dry statement of his main point in clear, simple language. His great gift for colorful colloquialism and storytelling cemented his appeal as an unaffected man of the people. Few could match him for the humorous tales that he used as parable, explanation, and analogy. When the grave issue of slavery's expansion shook the political system during the 1850s, however, he reined in his humor and surprised many with his ethical seriousness. A colleague remarked that, when thoroughly roused, Lincoln "would come out with an earnestness of conviction, a power of argument, a wealth of illustration, that I have never seen surpassed."

dent truth— Made so plain by our good Father in Heaven, that all feel and understand it, even down to brutes and creeping insects— The ant, who has toiled and dragged a crumb to his nest, will furiously defend the fruit of his labor, against whatever robber assails him— So plain, that the most dumb and stupid slave that ever toiled for a master, does constantly know that he is wronged— So plain that no one, high or low, ever does mistake it, except in a plainly selfish way; for although volume upon volume is written to prove slavery a very good thing, we never hear of the man who wishes to take the good of it, by being a slave himself—

Most governments have been based, practically, on the denial of the equal rights of men, as I have, in part, stated them; they began, by affirming those rights— They said, some men are too ignorant, and vicious, to share in government— Possibly so, said we; and, by your system, you would always keep them ignorant, and vicious— We proposed to give all a chance; and we expected the weak to grow stronger, the ignorant, wiser; and all better, and happier together—

We made the experiment; and the fruit is before us— Look at it— think of it— Look at it, in its aggregate grandeur, of extent of country, and numbers of population— of ship, and steamboat, and rail—

ABRAHAM LINCOLN

(1809–1865)

Autograph manuscript, speech fragment on slavery and government, ca. 1858
The Gilder Lehrman Institute of American History; GLC03251

These twenty-seven lines provide valuable insight into Lincoln's thought process at a crucial moment of his public life. He advances the fundamental truth that all creatures will fight for the fruits of their labor, drawing upon the kind of moral story he admired as a youthful reader of Aesop's fables. It illustrates his use of familiar parables to convey complex ideas to his audience.

ABRAHAM LINCOLN

(1809–1865)

Autograph manuscript, fragment of "House divided" speech, ca. 1858

The Gilder Lehrman Institute of American History; GLC02533

In what is believed to be Lincoln's earliest formulation of his "House Divided" doctrine, Lincoln identifies slavery as a moral and political issue that threatens the survival of the United States. Invoking the famous biblical phrase from Mark 3:25, "A house divided against itself can not stand," he declares, "I believe this government can not endure permanently, half slave, and half free." These words would have been particularly resonant in the mid-nineteenth century, when the Bible was almost universally familiar.

ABRAHAM LINCOLN

(1809–1865)

Autograph fragment of a speech, ca. 18 May–21 August 1858

The Morgan Library & Museum, purchased by Pierpont Morgan, ca. 1905; MA 230

These notes were composed for Lincoln's 1858 debates with his Democratic rival, Stephen Douglas, in the race for the United States Senate. In this fragment, Lincoln forcefully asserts a politician's obligation to provide moral leadership: "In this age, and this country, public sentiment is everything. With it, nothing can fail; against it, nothing can succeed. Whoever moulds public sentiment, goes deeper than he who enacts statutes, or pronounces judicial decisions." Lincoln condemns Douglas for ignoring the moral dimension of the slavery issue and attacks his position that "[slaves] have no part in the [D]eclaration of Independence . . . that slavery and liberty are perfectly consistent."

al question about slavery— that liberty and
slavery are perfectly consistent—indeed, necessary
accompaniments— that for a strong man to enslave himself the superior of a weak one, and
thereupon enslave the weak one, is the very ess-
ence of liberty,— the most sacred right of
self-government— When, I say, public sentiment shall be brought to all this, in the
name of heaven, what barriers will be left
against slavery being made lawful everywhere?
Can you find one word of his, opposed to it?
Can you not find many strongly favoring it?
If for his life— for his eternal salvation— he
was solely strong for that end, could he
find any means so well adapted to reach
the end?

If our Presidential election, by a mere plurality,
and of doubtful significance, brought our
Supreme court decision, that no power can exclude slavery from a Territory; how much
more, shall a public sentiment, in exact
accordance with the sentiments of Judge Douglas, bring another that no power can exclude
it from a State?

And then, the negro being doomed,
and damned, and forgotten, to everlasting
bondage, is the white man quite certain
that the tyrant demon will not turn upon
him too?

Welcome, or unwelcome, agreeable, or disagree-
able, whether this shall be an entire slave nation,
is the issue before us— Every incident— every little
shifting of scenes, or of actors— only clears away
the intervening trash, compacts and consolidates the
opposing hosts, and brings them more and more
distinctly face to face— The conflict will be a
severe one. and it will be fought through by those
who do care for the result, and not by those who do
not care— by those who are for, and those who
are against a legalized national slavery.— The
combined charge of Nebraskaism, and Dred Scottism

must be repulsed, and rolled back. The deceitful
cloak of "self-government" wherewith "the sum of
all villanies," seeks to protect and adorn itself,
must be torn from its hateful carcass. That
counterfeit upon judicial decision, and slander
and profanation upon the honored names, and
sacred history of republican America, must be
overruled, and expunged from the books of authority.

To give the victory to the right, not bloody, but-
lets, but peaceful ballots only, are necessary—
Thanks to our good old constitution, and organ-
ization under it, these alone are necessary— It only
needs that every right-thinking man, shall go to the
polls, and without fear or prejudice, vote as his think-

We are not enemies, but friends.
We must not be enemies.

ABRAHAM LINCOLN
4 March 1861

NATIONAL LEADER

One of Lincoln's greatest achievements was his articulation of a rationale for the Civil War and its sacrifices, shaped to inspire loyal Unionists. His leadership rested far less on coercion than on his faith in what he described as "the power of the right word from the right man to develop the latent fire and enthusiasm of the masses."

As president, he had only limited time for preparing substantial speeches. He spoke in public nearly a hundred times, but his remarks were usually modest and often unscripted. They included short addresses to troops, impromptu responses to well-wishers who came to "serenade" him, and statements to visiting delegations of, among others, clergymen, border-state representatives, and free blacks. Exceptions to this general rule included the two most celebrated speeches of his presidency, the Gettysburg Address and his second inaugural address. Significantly, they were his pithiest.

For these reasons Lincoln relied less on the spoken than the written word. Most effective of all were his carefully crafted and widely circulated public letters. He skillfully designed each to rally support on an issue crucial to the prosecution of the war: emancipation and racial issues, conscription, military arrests, and the suspension of habeas corpus.

ABRAHAM LINCOLN
(1809–1865)
Document, signed, Washington, DC,
Respite of execution for slaver Nathaniel Gordon, 4 February 1862
The Gilder Lehrman Institute of American History; GLC00182

This document stands out in the history of a man renowned for his mercy and willingness to forgive. His refusal to grant the condemned Nathaniel Gordon clemency for his capital crime made Lincoln the only American president to execute a slave trader. Predictably, Lincoln's decision caused a huge public stir. The execution made an example of Gordon to all slave traders, to the Confederacy, and to the world.

*We never hear of the man
who wishes to take the good of it,
by being a slave himself.*

ABRAHAM LINCOLN
ca. 1858–59

THE EMANCIPATOR

Lincoln felt strongly the injustice of slavery. "I am naturally anti-slavery," he wrote in 1864. "If slavery is not wrong, nothing is wrong. I can not remember when I did not so think, and feel." Yet he was careful never to describe it as a sin: Southerners were the victims of their particular circumstances. During the first year of the Civil War, to avoid scaring slave-owning loyalists in Kentucky and other border states, he had to be especially cautious when addressing slavery's future.

Federal setbacks during the first half of 1862 led Lincoln to take the radical step he called indispensable to national salvation. In the preliminary Emancipation Proclamation of 22 September, he pointedly used dry, legalistic language to declare—as commander in chief, guided by the Constitution—that on 1 January 1863, those held as slaves in still rebellious areas "shall be then, thenceforward, and forever free."

Lincoln thereafter crafted more refined language to place emancipation within the ethical rationale for the war. African Americans were implicit in his commitment at Gettysburg to "a new birth of freedom." When, in 1865, states began to ratify the emancipation amendment to the Constitution, he lauded this "King's cure for all the evils."

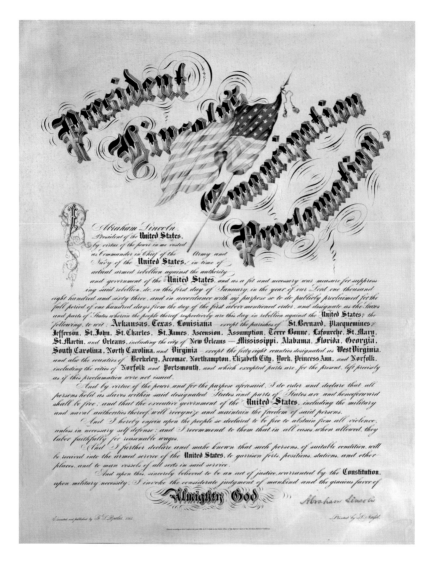

ABRAHAM LINCOLN

(1809–1865)

Document, signed, Washington, DC,

Emancipation Proclamation, 1 January 1863

The Gilder Lehrman Institute of American History; GLC00742

The Emancipation Proclamation was shaped by both pragmatic considerations and Lincoln's lifelong disdain for slavery. As a legal document, it aspires to precision rather than eloquence. Lincoln's use of county-specific terminology identified areas in rebellion, securing his proclamation as a wartime measure that would not be subject to judicial overthrow.

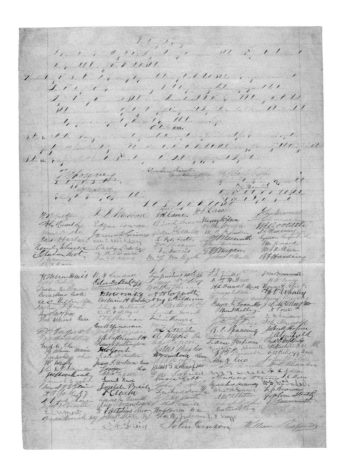

A Resolution submitting to the legislatures of the several States
a proposition to amend the Constitution of the United States, 38th Congress
[Second session, Washington, DC], 1865
The Morgan Library & Museum, purchased by Pierpont Morgan, 1908; MA 914

The Thirteenth Amendment declared that "Neither Slavery nor involuntary servitude, except as a punishment for crime, whereof the party shall have been duly convicted, shall exist within the United States." This was the first change made to the Constitution since 1804 and represents the first substantial expansion of civil liberties since the ratification of the Bill of Rights in 1791. It was the only ratified constitutional amendment signed by a president. Dated 8 April 1864, the date on which the resolution passed the Senate, this copy of the amendment, engrossed on vellum, is signed by Vice President Schuyler Colfax and members of Congress. It was countersigned by President Lincoln on 1 February 1865, emphatically signaling to the world his support of the abolition of slavery throughout the United States.

ABRAHAM LINCOLN

(1809–1865)

Autograph speech fragment, concerning the abolition of slavery, ca. 1858
The Gilder Lehrman Institute of American History; GLC05302

Lincoln encouraged Americans to look beyond politics and persevere in a good fight for a noble cause. With this speech he positioned himself within the international struggle over slavery, citing the example of British abolitionists William Wilberforce and Granville Sharpe. Lincoln's stark imagery subliminally links supporters of slavery with darkness and historical oblivion.

> *But I have also remembered that though they blazed, like tallow-candles for a century, at last they flickered in the socket, died out, stank in the dark for a brief season, and were remembered no more, even by the smell—School-boys know that Wilbe[r]force, and Granville Sharpe, helped that cause forward; but who can now name a single man who labored to retard it?*

ABRAHAM LINCOLN

(1809–1865)

Autograph manuscript, fragment
of annual message to Congress, 6 December 1864

The Gilder Lehrman Institute of American History; GLC08094

An amendment to end slavery had stalled in Congress in 1864. Aware that as commander in chief he had issued the Emancipation Proclamation as a temporary wartime measure, Lincoln led the attempt to abolish slavery forever through constitutional amendment. In this fragment of his last Annual Message—the equivalent of the current State of the Union address—he forcefully urges upon Congress "the reconsideration and passage of the [Thirteenth Amendment] at the present session." Lincoln's political leadership was never more evident.

ABRAHAM LINCOLN
(1809–1865)
Autograph letter, signed, Washington, DC,
to Horace Greeley, 24 March 1862
The Morgan Library & Museum,
Purchased by Pierpont Morgan before 1913; MA 6027

Lincoln had a fractious relationship with Greeley, the founding editor of the pro-Republican *New York Tribune*. But, given that the *Tribune*'s circulation was the largest in the country, he could not afford to alienate its editor. Lincoln's aide John Hay remarked that Greeley, a strident abolitionist, "grumbles because he is an honest old fanatic, and does not agree with the Administration; and all honest people honor him for his integrity, though they may differ by a world's width from his views." This letter shows Lincoln's respectfulness toward Greeley and illustrates how, with deliberate care, the president sought to win over his most vociferous opponents by arguing for a gradual approach, avoiding acrimony when possible— "persuasively, and not menacingly" are key terms.

With malice toward none,
with charity for all.

ABRAHAM LINCOLN
4 March 1865

V

HEALING A NATION

Lincoln was a kindly man, who by his own estimate probably had "too little" of the feeling of personal resentment—"a man has not time to spend half his life in quarrels," he reflected. He saw the irony that, as someone who did not bear a grudge, he had found himself at the center of such a profound conflict.

Lincoln's lifelong belief in America's national destiny and common purpose, however, led him to sanction an intensification of the war after the summer of 1862. It could no longer be fought, he said, "with elder stalk squirts charged with rosewater." His emancipation policy marked the end of conciliation, led to a developing assault on the South's people and economy, and prompted deep hostility in parts of the North.

As the end of this "hard war" approached, Lincoln sought to heal the wounds. At his second inauguration, with the Confederacy speedily crumbling, he called for a magnanimous postwar reconciliation. The crowd had expected the language of triumph; instead, he chose not to blame, spoke inclusively, emphasized the shared experience of—and God's judgment on—both sides in the conflict, and urged no vengeance toward the South. Of all Lincoln's words, these are the most transformative.

ABRAHAM LINCOLN

(1809–1865)
Pamphlet, Gettysburg Address, New York, 1863
The Gilder Lehrman Institute of American History; GLC05124

Four months after the Battle of Gettysburg, which caused 50,000 casualties—
soldiers dead, wounded, and missing—President Lincoln was invited to speak
at the dedication of a national cemetery at the site. A mere 275 words, Lincoln's
three-minute-long address redefined the significance of the Civil War. Drawing
upon biblical ideas of suffering, consecration, and resurrection, Lincoln framed the
war as a chapter in the modern struggle for self-government, liberty, and equality.
Considered at the time a sidebar to Senator Edward Everett's two-hour oration,
Lincoln's address soon emerged not only as the seminal event at Gettysburg but as
one of the most visionary speeches of the nineteenth century.

THE PRESIDENT'S

Dedication Address

AT GETTYSBURG.

FOUR score and seven years ago our fathers brought forth upon this continent a new nation, conceived in Liberty, and dedicated to the proposition that all men are created equal. Now we are engaged in a great civil war, testing whether that nation or any nation so conceived and so dedicated can long endure. We are met on a great battle-field of that war. We are met to dedicate a portion of it as the final resting-place of those who here gave their lives that that nation might live. It is altogether fitting and proper that we should do this. But in a larger sense we cannot dedicate, we cannot consecrate, we cannot hallow this ground. The brave men living and dead who struggled here have consecrated it far above our power to add or detract.

THE world will little note nor long remember what we say here, but it can never forget what they did here. It is for us, the living, rather to be dedicated here to the unfinished work that they have thus far so nobly carried on. It is rather for us to be here dedicated to the great task remaining before us, that from these honored dead we take increased devotion to that cause for which they here gave the last full measure of devotion; that we here highly resolve that the dead shall not have died in vain, that the nation shall, under God, have a new birth of freedom; and that governments of the people, by the people and for the people, shall not perish from the earth.

PUBLISHED BY MILLER & MATHEWS, 757 BROADWAY.

ABRAHAM LINCOLN

(1809–1865)

Autograph letter, signed, Washington, DC,
to Fanny McCullough, 23 December 1862
Shapell Legacy Partnership; SLP 346

The devastating losses of the Civil War made the composition of condolence letters one of Lincoln's regular, dismal duties. He wrote this deeply felt letter to the twenty-two-year-old Fanny McCullough only ten months after the death of his son Willie. Lincoln offers words of solace on the death of McCullough's father, telling her that "In this sad world of ours, sorrow comes to all; and, to the young, it comes with bitterest agony, because it takes them unawares. The older have learned to ever expect it. I am anxious to afford some alleviation of your present distress. Perfect relief is not possible, except with time. . . . I have had experience enough to know what I say; and you need only to believe it, to feel better at once."

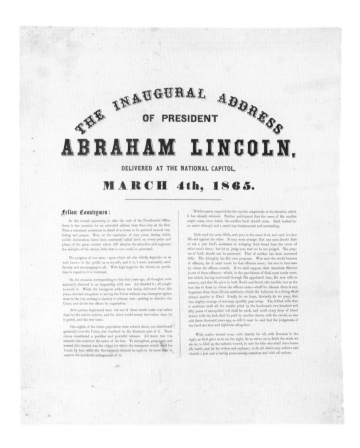

ABRAHAM LINCOLN

(1809–1865)

Broadside, Second inaugural address of President Abraham Lincoln,
Washington, DC, 4 March 1865
The Gilder Lehrman Institute of American History; GLC06044

Viewed by many as Lincoln's greatest speech, the second inaugural address declared that slavery was the war's essential cause and that the war was an expiation of the national sin of slavery. Speaking transcendently to history, and with a religious tone, President Lincoln explained the Civil War—its cause, its character, and its immediate consequences. Though he wanted to be clear that slavery caused "this mighty scourge of war," he ended on a hopeful note of binding up the nation's wounds. Lincoln's message of "charity for all" diverted some Republican desires for harsh retribution against the South.

This broadside is in blue ink and therefore was printed in the few weeks between the inauguration and the assassination. Copies printed after 15 April were in black ink, appropriate to the national mood of mourning.

I want you to cut the Knots,
and send them right along.

ABRAHAM LINCOLN
16 May 1861

VI

THE COMMANDER IN CHIEF

Lincoln was not a natural warrior. He had to learn about military command. As a lawyer, he knew how to draft lucid and cogent directions. As commander in chief, however, he was uncompromisingly clear in laying out strategy. When the security of Washington, DC, was threatened, Lincoln erupted at the bureaucratic delay and angrily ordered General Russell to move troops to Fort Monroe, 180 miles from the capital, exhorting: "I want you to cut the Knots, and send them right along."

Lincoln's words circulated in the military camps through publications that addressed the troops. He spoke to many volunteers individually. They admired the common touch of a president who lacked airs and graces, remained approachable, and mixed kindliness with good humor, jokes, and easy familiarity.

ABRAHAM LINCOLN

(1809–1865)

Autograph letter, signed, Washington, DC,
to Charles H. Russell, 16 May 1861

The Gilder Lehrman Institute of American History; GLC00635

Facing a crisis that threatened the security of Washington, DC, Lincoln erupts at
the bureaucratic delay and angrily orders General Charles H. Russell to move troops
to Fort Monroe, 180 miles from the capital: "I want you to cut the Knots and send
them right along." In his haste he mistakenly writes "Fort Sumpter" where he means
"Fort Monroe."

> *Learning today . . . that the order you have for forwarding the fourteen Regiments
> has something in it for the governor to do . . . , I am alarmed lest a <u>see-sawing</u>
> commences, by which neither your troops nor the Governor's will get along in any
> reasonable time. Now, I want you to cut the Knots, and send them right along—
> five Regiments here, and nine to Fort Sumpter, just as understood when we parted.*

Private

Executive Mansion,

Washington, March 26. , 1863.

Hon. Andrew Johnson
My dear Sir,

I am told you have at least thought of raising a negro military force. In my opinion the country now needs no specific thing so much as some man of your ability, and position, to go to this work. When I speak of your position, I mean that of an eminent citizen of a slave-state, and himself a slave-holder. The colored population is the great available and yet unavailed of, force for restoring the Union. The bare sight of fifty thousand armed, and drilled black soldiers on the banks of the Mississippi, would end the rebellion at once. And who doubts that we can present that sight, if we but take hold in earnest? If you have been thinking of it please do not dismiss the thought.

Yours truly
A. Lincoln

ABRAHAM LINCOLN

(1809–1865)

Autograph letter, signed, Washington, DC,
to Andrew Johnson, 26 March 1863
The Morgan Library & Museum, acquired by Pierpont Morgan, 1908; MA 810.8

Lincoln appointed Johnson military governor of Tennessee in March 1862, when much of the eastern part of the state remained under the control of rebel forces. Although Johnson was initially reluctant to recruit former slaves for the Union army—believing that they should continue to perform menial tasks, thus allowing white men to fight—Lincoln was aware that Johnson had "at least thought of raising a negro military force." In this letter, the president urges him to follow through, arguing that "the colored population is the great available and yet unavailed of, force for restoring the Union," and predicts that "the bare sight of fifty thousand armed, and drilled black soldiers on the banks of the Mississippi, would end the rebellion at once."

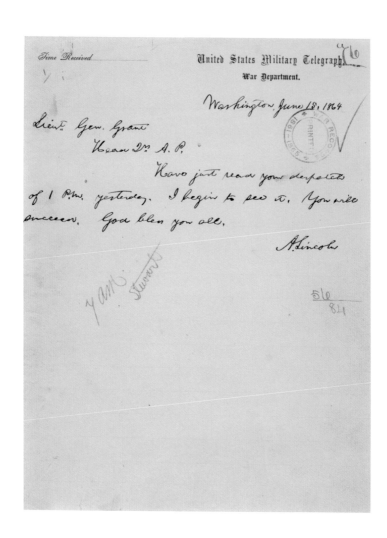

ABRAHAM LINCOLN

(1809–1865)
Autograph letter, signed, Washington, DC,
to Ulysses S. Grant, 15 June 1864
The Gilder Lehrman Institute of American History; GLC01572

Frustrated for years with the inaction and delays of his generals, Lincoln at last found a like-minded commander in Ulysses S. Grant. Writing tersely to avoid divulging details that could be intercepted, Lincoln telegraphed Grant to praise his strategy of total war: "I begin to see it. You will succeed."

My precious Boys and myself,
are left very desolate & brokenhearted.

MARY TODD LINCOLN
8 June 1865

VII

LINCOLN AMONG FRIENDS

Over the course of his career, Lincoln made many political and legal acquaintances, with some of whom he established close working relationships. His engaging conversation, capacious memory, and skillful storytelling made him entertaining company: more often than not he was the center of a crowd. As a private and self-reliant man, however, he had few intimate friends. Although his family provided emotional sustenance, his relations with his father were strained, his marriage to Mary was not always easy, and there was little intimacy with his eldest son, Robert.

Lincoln's surviving writings rarely allow us to see into his soul. Even so, his private correspondence reveals some personal exchanges. In the midst of the 1860 presidential campaign, Lincoln paused to write a letter of consolation to a friend of his son Robert, George C. Latham, who had been denied admission to Harvard. Lincoln wrote this letter of encouragement, declaring, "It is a <u>certain</u> truth that you <u>can</u> enter and graduate in Harvard University; and having made the attempt, you <u>must</u> succeed in it. '<u>Must</u>' is the word." Lincoln's words of encouragement to a young student offer an insight into his approach to making the most of his own life.

ABRAHAM LINCOLN

(1809–1865)

Autograph letter, signed, Springfield, Illinois, to Mary Owens, 7 May 1837

The Gilder Lehrman Institute of American History; GLC08085

In 1836, Lincoln found himself in a torturous situation. He felt obligated to his friend Elizabeth Abell to fulfill a promise to marry her sister, Mary Owens, if she came to Illinois from Kentucky. He regretted his rash promise and struggled to find an honorable way to get out of it. In this letter, he subtly discourages Mary by painting a bleak image of her future life with him and suggesting she could do better. In the end, when he proposed to Mary, she refused him.

Springfield, Ill. July 22. 1860.

My dear George

I have scarcely felt greater pain in my life than on learning yesterday from Bob's letter, that you had failed to enter Harvard University— And yet there is very little in it, if you will allow no feeling of discouragement to seize, and prey upon you— It is a certain truth that you can enter, and graduate in, Harvard University; and having made the attempt, you must succeed in it. "Must" is the word—

I know not how to aid you, save in the assurance of one of mature age, and much severe experience, that you can not fail, if you resolutely determine that you will not.

The President of the institution, can scarcely be other than a kind man; and doubtless he would grant you an interview, and point out the readiest way to remove, or overcome, the obstacles which have thwarted you—

In your temporary failure there is no evidence that you may not yet be a better scholar, and a more successful man in the great struggles of life, than many others, who have entered college more easily—

Again I say let no feeling of discouragement prey upon you, and in the end you are sure to succeed.

With more than a common interest I subscribe myself.

Very truly your friend.

A Lincoln.

ABRAHAM LINCOLN

(1809–1865)

Autograph letter, signed, Springfield, Illinois,
to George C. Latham, 22 July 1860

The Gilder Lehrman Institute of American History; GLC03876

In the midst of the 1860 presidential campaign, Lincoln paused to write a letter of consolation to a friend of his son Robert, George C. Latham, who had been denied admission to Harvard. Lincoln wrote this letter of encouragement declaring, "It is a certain truth that you can enter and graduate in Harvard University; and having made the attempt, you must succeed in it. 'Must' is the word." In the end Lincoln's kindness was not misplaced, although Latham went to Yale instead of Harvard.

ABRAHAM LINCOLN
(1809–1865)
Autograph letter, signed, City Point, Virginia,
to Mary Todd Lincoln, 2 April 1865
The Gilder Lehrman Institute of American History; GLC08090

At the greatest moment of his presidency—the fall of the Confederate capital, Richmond—Lincoln chose to write to his wife before writing to any public official. "Last night Gen. Grant telegraphed that Sheridan with his Cavalry and the 5th Corps have captured three brigades of Infantry, a train of wagons, and several batteries, prisoners amounting to several thousands. . . . " By tragic chance, this would prove to be the last letter he ever wrote to Mary.

MARY TODD LINCOLN

(1818–1882)

Autograph letter, signed, "near Chicago,"

to Mrs. Henry Wilson, 8 June 1865

The Morgan Library & Museum, purchased by Pierpont Morgan, 1906 or 1910; MA 810

———•———

This letter, written on customary mourning stationery less than two months after her husband's death, begins with an expression of Mrs. Lincoln's gratitude for the letter of condolence she had received from the wife of Senator Henry Wilson of Massachusetts. It provides a vivid insight into Mrs. Lincoln's emotional state early in her widowhood. She writes: "My precious Boys and myself, are left very desolate & brokenhearted, the deep waters of affliction have almost overwhelmed us and we find it very difficult, to bow in submission, to our Heavenly Father's will, the light of our life, has been taken away. . . . me, my Boys, are all deprived of their Counsellor & protector, my all, & the one, so devoted always to me, is removed from our sight forever!"

*Lincoln was one of the noblest wisest
and best men I ever knew.*

FREDERICK DOUGLASS
1880

VIII

LINCOLN IN THE EYES OF THE WORLD

Lincoln's horizons extended across the nineteenth-century world. Deeming the Union the "last, best hope of earth," he defined the Civil War as more than an American crisis. The struggle presented *"to the whole family of man,* the question, whether a constitutional republic . . . can, or cannot, maintain its territorial integrity, against its own domestic foes." Equally, the fight to end American slavery was part of a universal struggle between liberty and tyranny, social progress and lethargy.

Lincoln's public and private words encouraged progressives abroad to cast him as the embodiment of democratic freedom and modernity. His cruel death prompted a worldwide outpouring of grief. In Europe, grown men wept in the streets. The U.S. State Department was overwhelmed by a blizzard of tributes from every continent.

Foreign biographies suggest the extent of Lincoln's global reach. By 1900, he had become the subject of mostly admiring works published in German, French, Dutch, Italian, Portuguese, Greek, Spanish, Danish, Welsh, Hebrew, Russian, Norwegian, Finnish, Turkish, Swedish, and Japanese. Over the next quarter century, the list grew to include titles in Polish, Chinese, Czech, Arabic, Hungarian, Persian, Slovak, Armenian, and Korean. Variously seen as emancipator, nation builder, defender of representative government, and self-made man, Lincoln was a worldwide hero.

News of Lincoln's assassination took eleven days to reach London. This letter, by British actress and author Fanny Kemble, was written the day after she was told of Lincoln's death. Through her marriage to Pierce Butler (1807–1867), heir to vast plantations in the Carolinas and Georgia, Kemble had witnessed the atrocity of slavery firsthand. Her account was published in 1863 as *Journal of a Residence on a Georgian Plantation in 1838–1839,* and has been described as "a small masterpiece of generous outrage." Kemble's letter records the immediacy of her overwhelming shock and grief, and her anxiety about the future: "I cannot write I feel too incoherently all the horror & misery of this abominable crime—it is a southern deed—it represents the spirit of slaveholding."

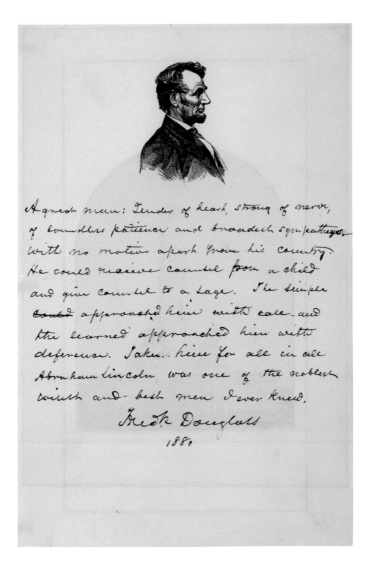

FREDERICK DOUGLASS

(1818–1895)

Autograph manuscript, signed, tribute to Lincoln, 1880

The Gilder Lehrman Institute of American History; GLC09091

Despite initial differences, Douglass and Lincoln forged a relationship over the course of the Civil War based on a shared vision. Fifteen years after Lincoln's death, Douglass described him as "one of the noblest wisest and best men I ever knew." This stirring tribute to Lincoln was later published in Osborn H. Oldroyd's *The Lincoln Memorial: Album-Immortelles* (1883).

Now he belongs to the ages.

EDWIN M. STANTON
15 April 1865

IX

A MAN FOR ALL TIME

Lincoln's words have lived on, thanks to their iteration by others as well as through their own intrinsic power. American political leaders, poets, playwrights, novelists, literary critics, theologians, journalists, and others have been inspired, challenged, and sometimes affronted by his sentiments.

Lincoln has also spoken—and continues to speak—to people throughout the world. Karl Marx judged him "the single-minded son of the working class." Tomas Masaryk, the first president of Czechoslovakia, drew strength as "the Lincoln of Central Europe." Racially mixed, republican Abraham Lincoln brigades fought in the Spanish Civil War. Mohandas Gandhi recognized in Lincoln a model of nonviolence. In Britain during the Second World War, his words stiffened resolve, while in Germany during the subsequent Cold War, West Berliners deployed Lincoln as a symbol of anticommunism and self-determination. At the same time, Ghanaians used him to legitimize liberation from British colonial rule and then to justify the new state's use of massive force against internal enemies. Recently Desmond Tutu accepted the Lincoln Leadership Prize for his role in national reconciliation in South Africa.

"Now he belongs to the ages," whispered the grieving secretary of war, Edwin M. Stanton, when Lincoln breathed his last. His words could scarcely have been more prescient.

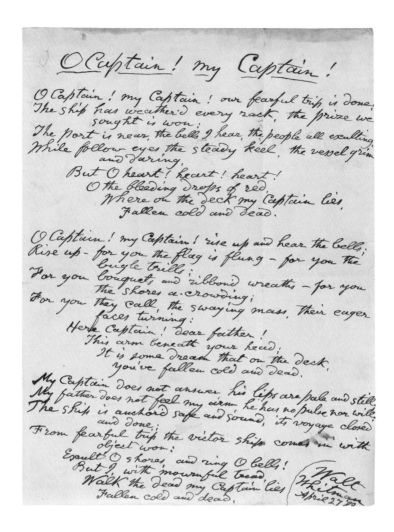

WALT WHITMAN

(1819–1892)

Autograph copy of "O Captain! My Captain!"

The Morgan Library & Museum, purchased in 1945; MA 1212.1

Lincoln's assassination inspired Walt Whitman to write this poem of mourning. It is
one of the few poems in which he used a conventional meter and rhyme scheme.
His tribute became extremely popular at the time of its first publication, in 1865, and
it was the only poem of Whitman's to be anthologized during his lifetime. In 1890,
ailing and in need of funds, Whitman was induced to write out this copy of his
famous poem for the distinguished Philadelphia physician, poet, and novelist Weir
Mitchell, who paid him $100 for it.

Lincoln Address
Feb 12 1909
Republican Club of New York City

which
You ask that he found a piece of property and turned into a free American citizen to speak to you to-night of Abraham Lincoln. I am not fitted by history or training to be your teacher to-night for, as I have stated, I was born a slave.

My first recollection of Abraham Lincoln was on this wise. I was awakened early one morning before the dawn of day as I lay wrapped in a bundle of rags on the dirt floor of our slave cabin by the prayers of my mother, just before leaving for the day's *as she* work, who was kneeling over my body earnestly praying that Abraham Lincoln might succeed and that one day she and her boy might be free. You give me an opportunity here this evening to celebrate with you and the Nation the answer to that prayer.

says the Great Book, Though a man die, yet shall he live. If this is true of the ordinary man, how much more true is it of the hero of the hour and the hero of the century--Abraham Lincoln.

One hundred years of the life and influence of Lincoln is but the repetition of the story of the struggles, the trials, ambitions and triumphs of those composing our complex American civilization. Interwoven into the warp and woof of it all is the graphic story of men and women of *nearly* every race and color, representing their progress from slavery to freedom, from poverty to wealth, from weakness to power, from ignorance to intelligence. Knit into the life of Abraham Lincoln is the story and success of the Nation in the blending of all tongues, religions, colors, races, into one composite Nation, leaving each group and race free to live its own separate social life and yet all a part of the great whole.

BOOKER T. WASHINGTON

(1856–1915)

Typed document, New York, New York, draft of speech, 12 February 1909
The Gilder Lehrman Institute of American History; GLC07232

In this 1909 tribute to Lincoln delivered to the Republican Club of New York City, Booker T. Washington remembers his mother on the dirt floor of their slave cabin praying that Lincoln would succeed in ending slavery. Now a prominent public figure, the former slave Washington sees Lincoln's legacy as the "blending of all tongues, religions, colors, races into one composite Nation."

"Liberty And Freedom
Shall Not Perish"
A. Lincoln

COLORED MEN
The First Americans
Who Planted
Our Flag
on the
Firing Line

TRUE SONS OF FREEDOM

...*we here highly resolve that these dead shall not have died in vain*...

REMEMBER DEC. 7th!

After the Japanese attack on Pearl Harbor in December 1941, many turned again to Lincoln for inspiration. This poster with its damaged but enduring star-spangled banner flying at half-staff features an excerpt from Lincoln's Gettysburg Address. The resilience and courage of Lincoln's words were much needed as the nation stirred itself to overcome this shocking attack and enter the fight against totalitarianism.

SELECT BIBLIOGRAPHY

Brookhiser, Richard, *Founders' Son: A Life of Abraham Lincoln,* New York, 2014.

Carwardine, Richard, *Lincoln: A Life of Purpose and Power,* New York, 2006.

Charyn, Jerome, *I Am Abraham,* New York, 2014.

Delbanco, Andrew, *The Portable Abraham Lincoln,* New York, 2009.

Donald, David Herbert, *Lincoln,* New York, 1995.

Foner, Eric, *The Fiery Trial: Abraham Lincoln and American Slavery,* New York, 2010.

———, *Our Lincoln: New Perspectives on Lincoln and His World,* New York, 2008.

Goodwin, Doris Kearns, *Team of Rivals: The Political Genius of Abraham Lincoln,* New York, 2006.

Guelzo, Allen C., *Abraham Lincoln as a Man of Ideas,* Carbondale, IL, 2009.

———, *Lincoln's Emancipation Proclamation: The End of Slavery in America,* New York, 2004.

———, *Lincoln: A Very Short Introduction,* New York, 2009.

Holzer, Harold, *Lincoln and the Power of the Press: The War for Public Opinion,* New York, 2014.

———, ed. *The Lincoln Anthology: Great Writers on His Life and Legacy from 1860 to Now,* New York, 2009.

Kaplan, Fred, *Lincoln: The Biography of a Writer,* New York, 2010.

McPherson, James M., *Tried by War: Abraham Lincoln as Commander in Chief,* New York, 2008.

Reynolds, David S., ed., *Lincoln's Selected Writings,* New York, 2014.

Samuels, Shirley, ed., *The Cambridge Companion to Abraham Lincoln,* New York, 2012.

White, Ronald C., *The Eloquent President: A Portrait of Lincoln Through His Words,* New York, 2004.

Wilson, Douglas, *Lincoln's Sword: The Presidency and the Power of Words,* New York, 2006.

CREDITS

PUBLISHED BY
THE MORGAN LIBRARY & MUSEUM

Karen Banks, *Publications Manager*
Patricia Emerson, *Senior Editor*
Eliza Heitzman, *Editorial Assistant*

PROJECT STAFF
Marilyn Palmeri, *Imaging and Rights Manager*
Graham S. Haber, *Photographer*
Eva Soos, *Imaging and Rights Assistant Manager*
Kaitlyn Krieg, *Imaging and Rights Administrative
    Assistant*
Janny Chiu, *Digital Photography Production
    Assistant*

Designed by Bessas & Ackerman
Typeset in Fairfield
Printed on Endurance Silk Text and bound by
    Puritan Capital, Hollis, New Hampshire

Professor Richard Carwardine
President, Corpus Christi College, Oxford

Declan Kiely
Robert H. Taylor Curator and Department Head
Literary and Historical Manuscripts
The Morgan Library & Museum

Sandra M. Trenholm
Curator of the Gilder Lehrman Collection
The Gilder Lehrman Institute of American History

AUTHORS' ACKNOWLEDGMENTS

At the Morgan Library & Museum: Pamela
Abernathy, John Alexander, Karen Banks,
Linden Chubin, Alex Confer, James Donchez,
Patricia Emerson, Rebecca Filner, Peggy Fogelman,
Simone Grant, Graham Haber, Eliza Heitzman,
Patrick Milliman, Christine Nelson, Christina Lee
Padden, Marilyn Palmeri, Michelle Perlin, Marie
Trope-Podell, Paula Pineda, Stephen Saitas, Tom
Shannon, Reba Fishman Snyder, Frank Trujillo,
Ian Umlauf, Carolyn Vega, and Scott Whipkey.

At the Gilder Lehrman Institute of American History:
Justine Ahlstrom, Tim Bailey, James Basker, Alinda
Borell, Beth Huffer, Susan Saidenberg, Professor
Douglas Wilson (Co-director, Lincoln Studies
Center at Knox College).